Starting off with
Adding and Subtracting

Written by Peter Patilla

Illustrations by Liz Pichon

OXFORD
UNIVERSITY PRESS

OXFORD

UNIVERSITY PRESS

Great Clarendon Street, Oxford OX2 6DP

Oxford University Press is a department of the University of Oxford.
It furthers the University's objective of excellence in research, scholarship,
and education by publishing worldwide in

Oxford New York

Athens Auckland Bangkok Bogotá Buenos Aires Calcutta
Cape Town Chennai Dar es Salaam Delhi Florence Hong Kong Istanbul
Karachi Kuala Lumpur Madrid Melbourne Mexico City Mumbai
Nairobi Paris São Paulo Singapore Taipei Tokyo Toronto Warsaw

with associated companies in Berlin Ibadan

Oxford is a registered trade mark of Oxford University Press
in the UK and in certain other countries

British Library Cataloguing in Publication Data available

H/b ISBN 0–19–910667–3
P/b ISBN 0–19–910668–1

1 3 5 7 9 10 8 6 4 2

Designed and Typeset by Perry Tate Design
Printed in Hong Kong

My name is

....

Notes for parents and teachers

This book develops and extends early concepts of *adding and subtracting* for adults and children to enjoy and share together. It has been carefully written to introduce key words and ideas that children will meet in their first couple of years in school.

Throughout the book, you will see **Word Banks** which contain the new mathematical words introduced for each concept. All the words from the word banks are gathered together at the back of the book. You can use the word banks with your child in several ways:

- See which of the words they recognized through games such as I spy. *I spy the word plus – can you find it? I spy a word beginning with m – where is it?*
- Choose a word and ask your child to find it in the book.
- Let your child choose a word and say something about it.

Look for other opportunities in everyday life to use the ideas and vocabulary introduced in this book. Add up sums of money, count how many knives and forks there are altogether, or total dice scores. Ensure your child realizes that addition and subtraction are easy, and most importantly, fun.

Adding and totalling

Putting sets together is the same as adding. This sign means add **+**.

Adding makes a set larger.

 **+**

3 ladybirds

2 bees

Altogether there are 5 insects.

 **+**

4 green planets

3 purple planets

Altogether there are 7 planets.

 **+**

6 add 4 makes 10.

What is the total number of birds?

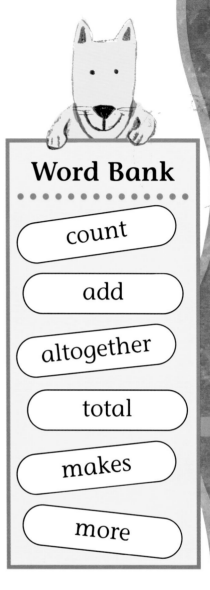

Word Bank

count

add

altogether

total

makes

more

What is the total number of ice creams?

What is the total number of dinosaurs?

Taking away and subtracting

Taking away is the same as subtracting.
This sign means subtract — .

Taking away makes a set smaller.

5 take away 2 leaves 3.   6 remove 1 leaves 5.

8 take away 2 leaves 6.

9 subtract 3 leaves 6.

How many have left the bowl?
How many stay behind?

How many are leaving?
How many stay behind?

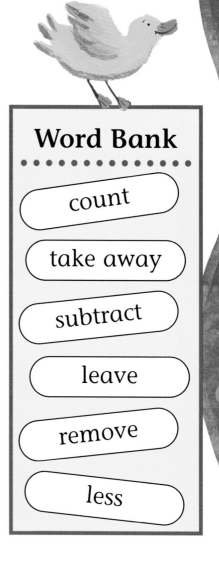

Word Bank

- count
- take away
- subtract
- leave
- remove
- less

2 ducks fly away.
How many will be left?

3 fish are eaten.
How many will that leave?

How many more?

Comparing sets tells us which one has more.

You can find out how many more by counting on.
Count on from the smaller number.

5 is 2 more than 3.

4 is 2 more than 2.

7 is 3 more than 4.

5 green snails.

8 purple snails.

There are more purple snails than green snails. There are 3 more.

Tom

Who has more bricks?
How many more?

Joe

Who has made the longer line?
How many more are needed to make
them the same?

Fran

Ben

Who has the higher score?
How many more?

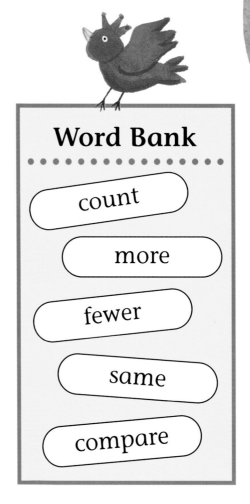

Word Bank

count

more

fewer

same

compare

Jumping along and adding

We can use a number track to help with adding.

Jumping forwards along a number track is the same as adding on.

Frog was on 5 and jumped forwards 2.

5 + 2 makes 7

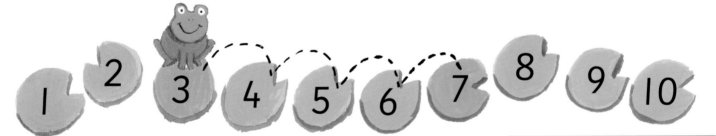

Frog is on 3. She will make 4 jumps.

3 + 4 makes 7

Frog is on 6. To reach 10 she must make 4 jumps.

6 + 4 makes 10

3 + 2
Where do you start?
How many jumps?
Where do you end?

10
9
8
7
6
5
4
3
2
1

5 + 4
Where do you start?
How many jumps?
Where do you end?

1
2
3
4
5
6
7
8
9
10

Start on 4.
Jump to 10.
How many jumps?

Word Bank

count on   makes

add   forwards

Jumping back and subtracting

We can use a number track to help with subtracting.

Jumping back along a number track is the same as subtracting or taking away.

Bee started on 5 and jumped back 2.

5 – 2 leaves 3

Bee was on 7. She made 4 jumps back.

7 – 4 is 3

Bee is on 10. To reach 4 she must make 6 jumps.

10 – 6 reaches 4

10
9
8
7
6
5
4
3
2
1

6 – 4
Where do you start?
How many jumps?
Where do you end?

Start on 9.
Jump to 4.
How many jumps?

1
2
3
4
5
6
7
8
9
10

10 – 6
Where do you start?
How many jumps?
Where do you end?

Word Bank

count back

backwards

subtract

take away

leaves

Plus and equals

We use these two signs when we are adding, **+** and **=** .

+ is the plus sign.   **=** is the equals sign.

The plus sign tells us to add.

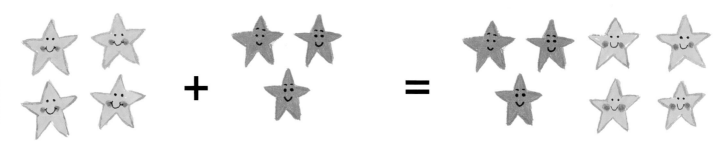

Four plus three equals seven.

$$4 + 3 = 7$$

Two and seven more makes nine.

$$2 + 7 = 9$$

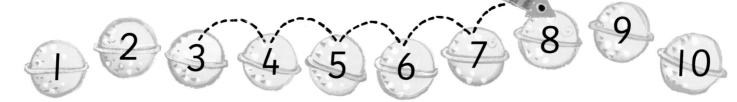

Three jump along five reaches eight.

$$3 + 5 = 8$$

$3 + 5 = 8$ is a sum

3 + 5 = 8

5 + 3 = 8

It does not matter which number you add first.
It is quicker to count on from the larger number.

Adder visits each set and adds 4.
How many will be in each set after the visit?
Write a sum for each visit.

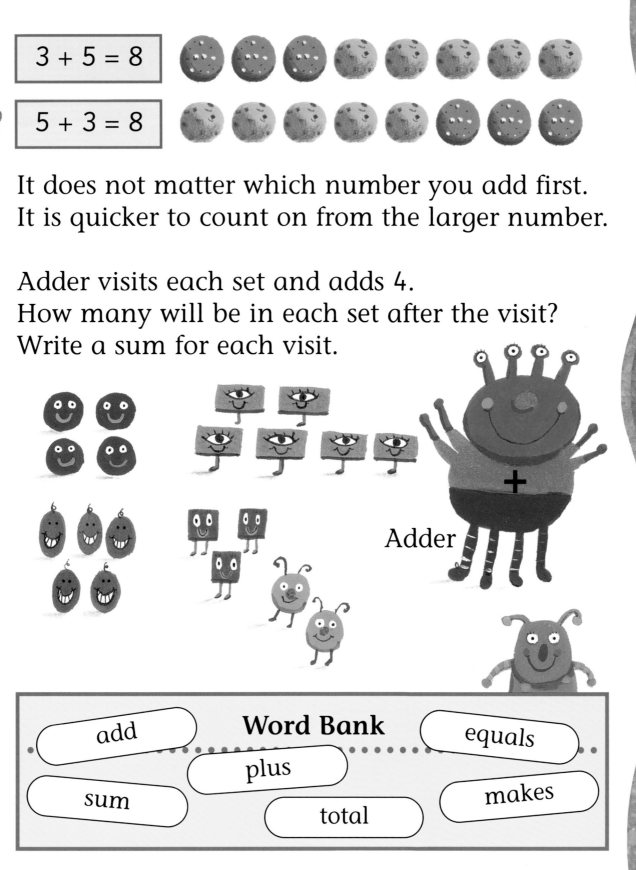

Adder

Word Bank

add   equals

plus

sum   makes

total

Minus and equals

We use these two signs when we are subtracting, − and = .

− is the minus sign.   = is the equals sign.

The minus sign tells us to subtract.

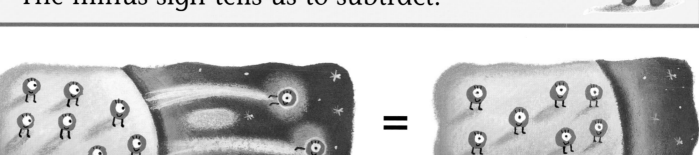

Nine take away two   equals seven. $9 - 2 = 7$

  =

Six take away two   equals four. $6 - 2 = 4$

Ten jump back four is six. $10 - 4 = 6$

$10 - 4 = 6$ is a subtraction

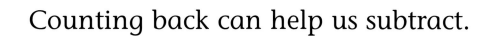

Counting back can help us subtract.

$$6 - 4 = 2$$

6 count back 4 lands on 2.

Nipper visits each set and takes away 4.
How many will be in each set after the visit?
Write a subtraction sum for each visit.

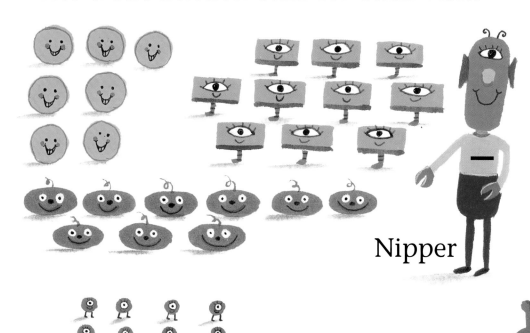

Nipper

Word Bank

subtract

minus

equals

take away

leaves

less

Adding machines

Number machines change numbers.
Adding machines make numbers larger.

Numbers go into the adding machine.
The machine changes the number.
The answer comes out of the machine.

4 enters the machine.
It adds on 3.
7 will leave the machine.

2 enters the machine.
It adds on 4.
6 will leave the machine.

Jumping along the number track will help you add on.

0 1 2 3 4 5 6 7 8 9 10

Which numbers will leave each of these machines?

Word Bank

add

equals

enter

total

leave

plus

Subtraction machines

Number machines change numbers.
Subtraction machines make numbers smaller.

Numbers go into the take away machine.
The machine changes the number.
The answer comes out of the machine.

4 enters the machine.
It takes away 1.
3 will leave the machine.

5 enters the machine.
It takes away 2.
3 will leave the machine.

Jumping back on the number track will help you subtract.

| 0 | 1 | 2 | 3 | 4 | 5 | 6 | 7 | 8 | 9 | 10 |

Which numbers will leave each of these machines?

Word Bank

subtract   minus

enter   take away   leave   equals

The story of 10

$1 + 9 = 10$

$2 + 8 = 10$

$3 + 7 = 10$

$4 + 6 = 10$

$5 + 5 = 10$

$6 + 4 = 10$

$7 + 3 = 10$

$8 + 2 = 10$

$9 + 1 = 10$

$10 + 0 = 10$

22

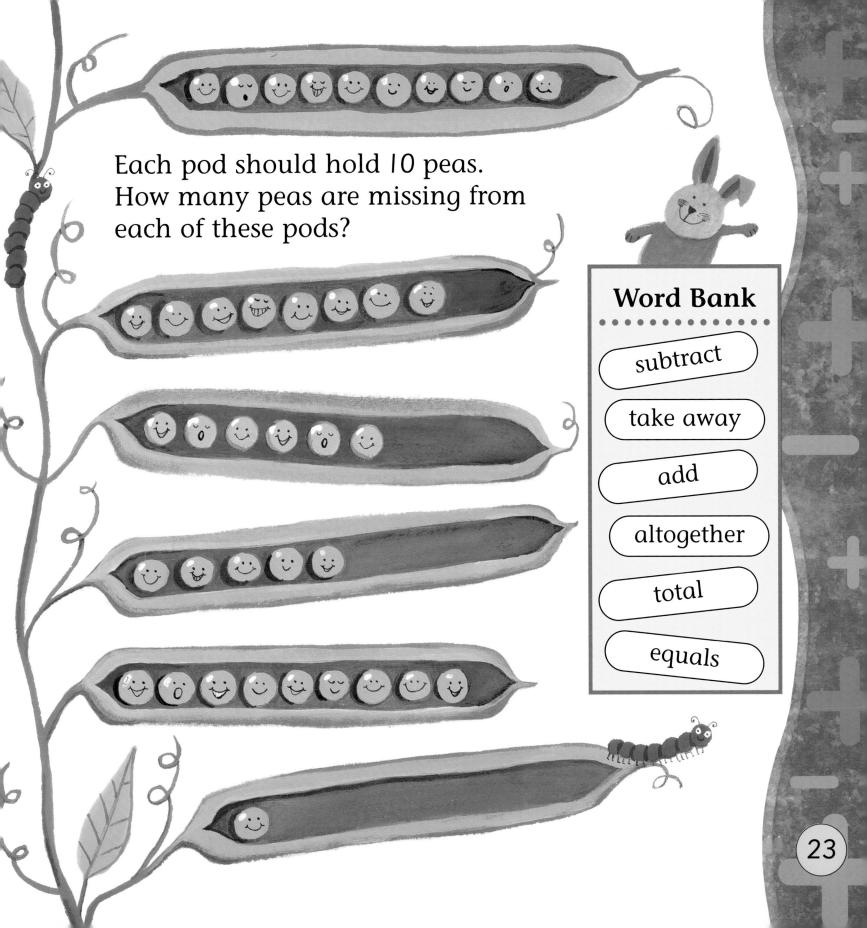

Each pod should hold 10 peas.
How many peas are missing from
each of these pods?

Word Bank

subtract

take away

add

altogether

total

equals

23

Counting on and back

We can add to large numbers.
Counting on will find the total.
We can subtract from large numbers.
Counting back will find the answer.

1 2 3 4 5 6 7 8 9 10 11 12 13 14 15 16 17 18 19 20

| 12 + 2 = | 17 − 2 = |

Start on 12.
Make 2 jumps forward.
You land on 14.
12 + 2 = 14

Start on 17.
Make 2 jumps back.
You land on 15.
17 − 2 = 15

Jumping forward is the same as adding.

Jumping back is the same as subtracting.

Use the number track to help you add and subtract.

Add on 2 to each of these numbers.

16   10   12   13   18

Subtract 3 from each of these numbers.

17   13   15   16   20

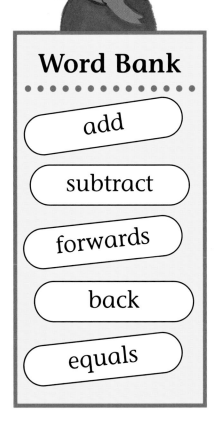

Word Bank

- add
- subtract
- forwards
- back
- equals

Using zero

Zero is the number 0.
We sometimes call it nought or nothing.

Adding zero, or nothing, to any number does not change it.

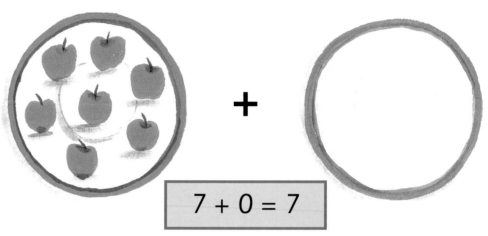

$$7 + 0 = 7$$

Subtracting zero, or nothing, from any number does not change it.

$$5 - 0 = 5$$

Word Bank

zero

adding

nought

nothing

subtracting

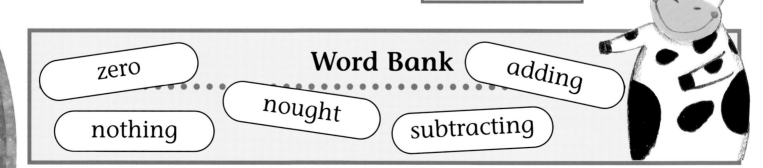

Did you know?

The signs **+ −** and **=** have been used for hundreds of years.

+ was written on sacks of grain that were too heavy.

− was written on sacks of grain that were too light.

The first mathematician to use = was Robert Recorde.

1	2	3	4	5
6	7	8	9	10

The numbers we use to write sums came from India a long time ago.

Word Bank

Do you remember these words?
Can you find them in the book?

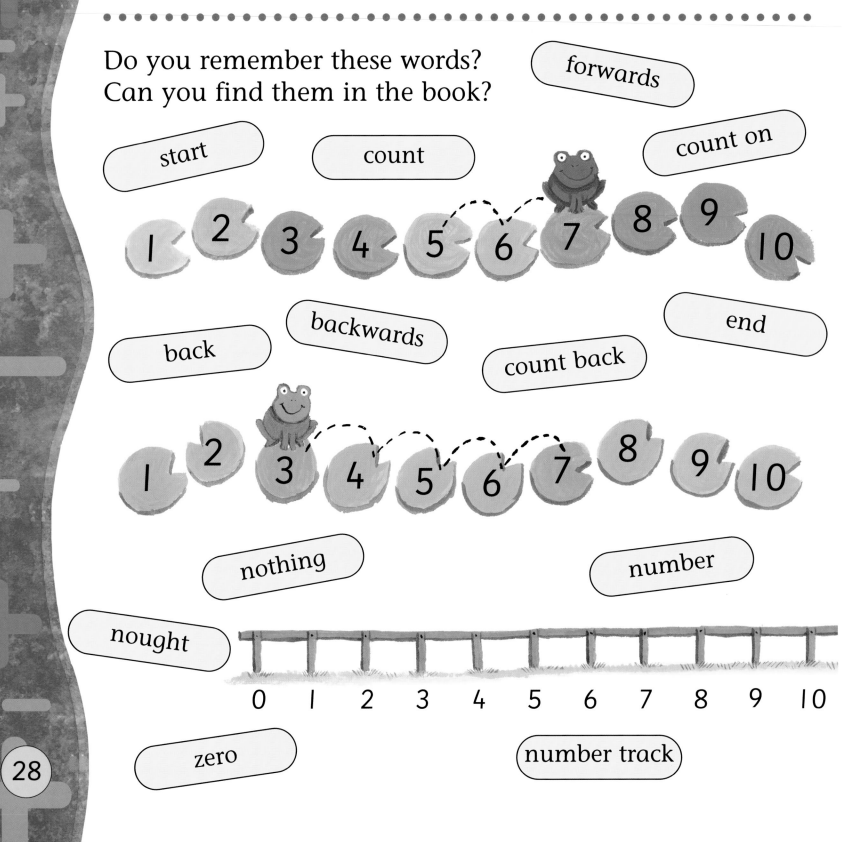

forwards

start

count

count on

back

backwards

count back

end

nothing

number

nought

zero

number track

Word Bank

same

pairs

larger

how many?

compare

less

more

score

Word Bank

subtraction

minus

subtracting

−2

3

5

leaves

take away

remove

subtract

leave

fewer

Word Bank

sum

makes

altogether

sign

totalling

plus

equals

add

total

adding

enter

+3

7

4

Adding and Subtracting Quiz

What is the score?

If 4 fly away how many will be left?

How many more has Luke?

Luke   Carla

What is the total?

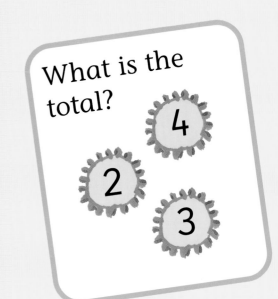

What is left if you take away 0 from 6?

There should be 10 peas in the pod. How many are missing?